Adam Levine

ABDO
Publishing Company

Big
Buddy BOOKS
Buddy Bios

by Sarah Tieck

VISIT US AT
www.abdopublishing.com

Published by ABDO Publishing Company, PO Box 398166, Minneapolis, Minnesota 55439.

Printed in the United States of America, North Mankato, Minnesota.
052013
092013

 PRINTED ON RECYCLED PAPER

Coordinating Series Editor: Rochelle Baltzer
Contributing Editors: Megan M. Gunderson, Marcia Zappa
Graphic Design: Maria Hosley
Cover Photograph: *AP Photos*: Brian Lindensmith/Patrick McMullan/Sipa USA (Sipa via AP Images).
Interior Photographs/Illustrations: *AP Photos*: Kevork Djansezian (pp. 15, 17), Scott Gries (p. 21), Kiichiro Sato (p. 13), Matt Sayles (pp. 23, 25), John Shearer/Invision for Citi, John Shearer, file (p. 5); *Getty Images*: Jerritt Clark/WireImage (p. 19), Charley Gallay/Getty Images for Westfield (p. 7), Jeff Kravitz/FilmMagic (p. 11), Kevin Mazur/WireImage (p. 26), Christopher Polk/Getty Images for A&M/Octone (p. 18), Adam Taylor/NBC/NBCU Photo Bank via Getty Images (p. 29), Noel Vasquez (p. 7), WireImage (p. 9); *Glow Images*: © Josh Gosfield/Corbis/Glow Images (p. 21); *Shutterstock*: Melinda Fawver (p. 12).

Library of Congress Control Number: 2012956009

Cataloging-in-Publication Data

Tieck, Sarah.
 Adam Levine: famous singer & songwriter / Sarah Tieck.
  p. cm. -- (Big buddy biographies)
 ISBN 978-1-61783-859-0
 1. Levine, Adam, 1979- --Juvenile literature. 2. Singers--United States--Biography--Juvenile literature.   I. Title.
 782.42164092--dc23
 [B]   2012956009

Contents

Rock Star

Adam Levine is best known as the lead singer of the band Maroon 5. He also writes songs and plays **guitar**. And, he is a **coach** on the television show *The Voice*.

Oregon

California | Nevada

PACIFIC OCEAN

Arizona

Los Angeles

Family Ties

Adam Noah Levine was born in Los Angeles, California, on March 18, 1979. His parents are Fred Levine and Patsy Noah. His brother is Michael.

When Adam was seven, his parents split. He grew up spending time with both parents. Adam has a stepsister named Julia. He also has a half sister, Liza, and a half brother, Sam.

Adam spends time with his mom (*left*), and also with his dad and brother Michael (*above*). Sometimes they get to attend events together.

Early Years

Adam enjoyed music from a young age. In junior high, he and friends Jesse Carmichael and Mickey Madden played music together at a school dance.

Adam liked playing music, but he was very shy. The first time he performed, he turned his back to the crowd.

Adam saw the rock group Warrant play when he was in fifth grade. This was his first concert.

9

Adam attended Brentwood School in Los Angeles. He, Jesse, and Mickey formed a band with their friend Ryan Dusick. They called it Kara's Flowers.

In 1997, they **released** the album *The Fourth World*. One of its songs was "Soap Disco." That year, Kara's Flowers even appeared on the television show *Beverly Hills 90210*. Shortly after, the group broke up.

Jesse, Mickey, Adam, and Ryan (*left to right*) later formed the band Maroon 5.

Many entertainers live and work in Los Angeles.

School Days

After high school, Adam attended Five Towns College in Long Island, New York. There, he heard different types of music. These included **rhythm and blues**, **hip-hop**, and **soul**.

Adam left New York before finishing college. He returned to Los Angeles with many new ideas for his music.

Adam and Jesse attended
Five Towns College together.

Starting Out

Around 2000, the members of Kara's Flowers formed a new band. They added James Valentine on **guitar**. They named the band Maroon 5. People especially noticed the group's new sound.

In 2002, Maroon 5 **released** their first album, *Songs About Jane*. Popular songs included "Harder to Breathe," "She Will Be Loved," and "This Love." Over the next two years, the band played many shows. Their album became a hit!

In 2005, Maroon 5 won a Grammy Award for Best New Artist. In 2006, they won another Grammy for "This Love."

15

Big Break

Adam and Maroon 5 worked to grow their success. In 2006, Ryan Dusick left the band. Matt Flynn replaced him as drummer. In 2007, Maroon 5 **released** the album *It Won't Be Soon Before Long*. It was a hit!

One of the album's songs was "Makes Me Wonder." In just a week, the song went from number 64 to number 1 on the Billboard Hot 100. At the time, this set a record! And, it was the band's first number one song.

Maroon 5 continued to work on new music. In 2010, they **released** *Hands All Over*. The songs "Misery" and "Moves Like Jagger" became very popular.

In 2012, Maroon 5 released *Overexposed*. "Payphone" and "Daylight" were hit songs from that album.

"Moves Like Jagger" featured Christina Aguilera with Maroon 5. They worked together to make a music video for the song.

Fans often ask Adam for his autograph.

Yoga Master

Adam enjoys doing yoga. Yoga trains the mind and body by stretching and moving through poses. Adam says yoga helps him on stage and in his life.

Adam has made videos showing his yoga practice. He says he can focus better from doing yoga. And, he says it makes him a more successful musician.

Half moon is one of Adam's favorite yoga poses.

Adam practices yoga for at least one hour before performing a concert.

21

TV Star

In 2011, Adam had become a judge and **coach** on *The Voice*. This television show finds talented singers. Adam and three other judges choose the finalists. This took Adam's work and talents in a new direction.

Adam worked with host Carson Daly and coaches CeeLo Green, Christina Aguilera, and Blake Shelton on the first three seasons of *The Voice*.

A Singer's Life

As a singer and songwriter, Adam spends time working on songs for Maroon 5. He and his bandmates go to recording studios to make albums.

After Maroon 5 albums come out, Adam works hard to promote them. He appears on television and in magazines. And, he performs live for fans. He and Maroon 5 may travel for several months on a concert tour.

Adam often works with other singers and musicians. He performed "Stereo Hearts" with Gym Class Heroes at the 2011 American Music Awards.

In 2010, Adam and other singers helped raise money after the earthquake in Haiti. They recorded "We Are the World 25 for Haiti."

Did you know...

Adam has ADHD. He has worked to manage it.

Off the Stage

Family is important to Adam. When he is not working, he spends time with his family and friends. Adam also enjoys being at home. He is known for his decorating style.

Adam likes to help others. He works to raise awareness for causes he cares about. These include **ADHD**, **cancer**, and gay rights.

Buzz

In 2013, Adam toured with Maroon 5 to **promote** *Overexposed*. He also worked on season four of *The Voice*. He helped the show's singers improve their skills.

Adam's fame continues to grow. Fans are excited to see what's next for him!

Shakira and Usher joined Adam and Blake as coaches on season four of *The Voice*.

I WANT YOU

I WANT YOU

29

Snapshot

★**Name**: Adam Noah Levine

★**Birthday**: March 18, 1979

★**Birthplace**: Los Angeles, California

★**Albums**: *The Fourth World (as Kara's Flowers), Songs About Jane, It Won't Be Soon Before Long, Hands All Over, Overexposed*

★**Appearances**: *Beverly Hills 90210, The Voice*

Important Words

ADHD attention deficit/hyperactivity disorder. A condition in which a person has trouble paying attention, sitting still, or controlling actions.

cancer any of a group of very harmful diseases that cause a body's cells to become unhealthy.

coach someone who teaches or trains a person or a group on a certain subject or skill.

guitar (guh-TAHR) a stringed musical instrument played by strumming.

hip-hop a form of popular music that features rhyme, spoken words, and electronic sounds. It is similar to rap music.

perform to do something in front of an audience.

promote to help something become known.

release to make available to the public.

rhythm and blues (RIH-thuhm) a form of popular music that features a strong beat. It is inspired by jazz, gospel, and blues styles.

soul a form of music created by African Americans. It expresses deep feeling and includes gospel and rhythm and blues styles.

Web Sites

To learn more about Adam Levine, visit ABDO Publishing Company online. Web sites about Adam Levine are featured on our Book Links page. These links are routinely monitored and updated to provide the most current information available.

www.abdopublishing.com

Index